Sunny's Time to Tell!

A Book about Tattling, Telling, and Personal Safety

Written by Julie Mendenhall

Illustrated by Maja Sommersted

"Sunny's Time to Tell: A Book about Tattling, Telling, and Personal Safety"

youth light
inc.

© 2014 YouthLight, Inc.
PO Box 115
Chapin, SC 29036
800-209-9774
www.youthlight.com

Cover Artwork and Illustrations by: Maja Sommersted
Layout and Design by: Melanie Butler

ISBN: 978-1-59850-146-9
Library of Congress Control Number: 2013952399

10 9 8 7 6 5 4 3 2 1
Printed in the United States

A Word from the Author

As an elementary school counselor, I know it is not easy to develop awareness in our children on sensitive subjects. I developed this book in order to give others a guide on how to share critical information to children on the important issues of tattling, telling, and personal safety.

Content within this book is annotated and/or contains factual referencing. These references are denoted by a  symbol and can be found in the Appendix at the back of this book. Important words or phrases are denoted by either **red** or **green** lettering, and extended information for older children appears in **blue**.

Thank you to those who have supported and encouraged me to continue this endeavor. Thank you to the children and adults who have shared their stories. One needs to stand firm and speak up to prevent abuse.

We need to encourage others to tell.

Sincerely,

Julie Mendenhall

Hi there!
My name is Sunny.

I like it when people
say "Hi" to me.

Say, "Hi Sunny!"

Thanks, that makes me feel good.

Most of the time, I'm full of sunshine, cheerful and happy.

But sometimes I'm sad and don't feel so good inside.

When I'm sad or hurting I'm not sunshiny anymore.

I get dark and cloudy depending on how I feel.

Like when someone tattles on me.

5

I want to talk with you about
the difference between tattling and telling.

But first I want to hear what you think.

What is the difference between
tattling and telling?

Do you know?

Here, let me share the difference with you.

Tattling is when:
- ✓ It's not that important
- ✓ You can solve it by yourself
- ✓ You just want to get someone in trouble
- ✓ No one is hurt
- ✓ It was an accident
- ✓ It's not dangerous

Telling is when:
- ✓ It is really important
- ✓ You used your words, but they won't stop
- ✓ Someone could get hurt
- ✓ Someone is in danger
- ✓ It is not safe

I would be tattling if I went straight to an adult before saying anything to the person who was teasing me.

We could...
Look at them, Name It,
and Walk Away.
We could...
Stop, Walk, and Talk.

But if they keep bothering us,
then it is time to tell.
That's okay, especially after
we tried to use our words.

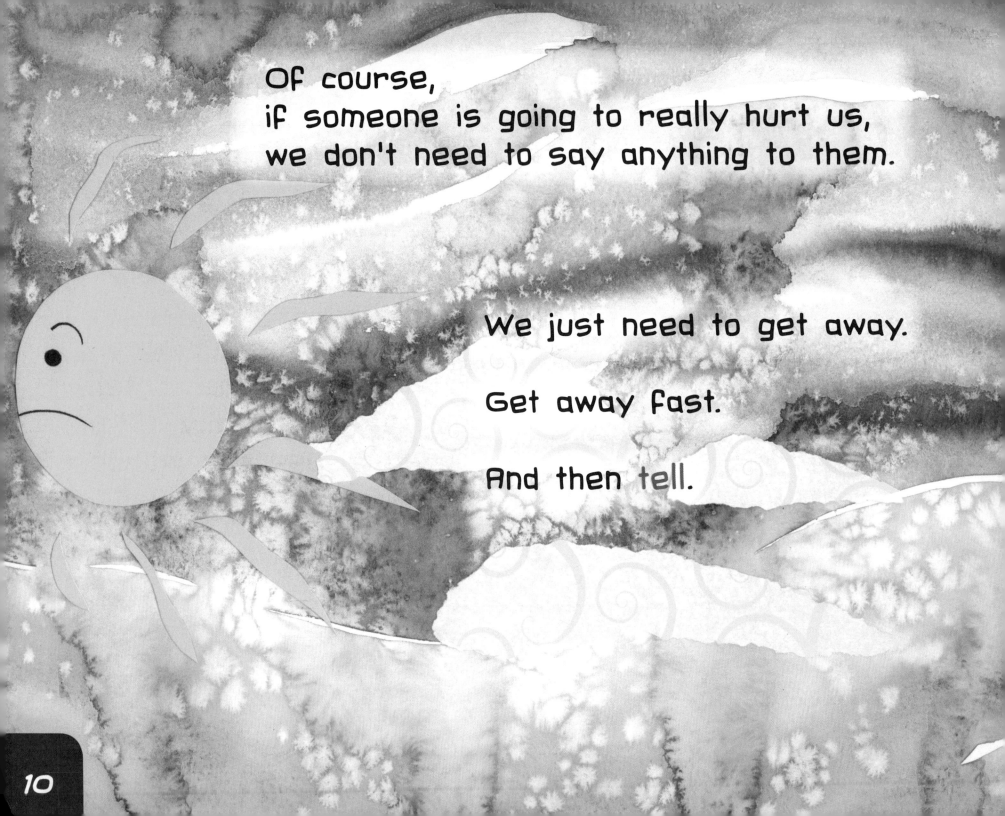

Of course,
if someone is going to really hurt us,
we don't need to say anything to them.

We just need to get away.

Get away fast.

And then tell.

Deep inside I know when telling is important.

Again,
let's look at the telling list.
We should tell someone when:
- ✓ It's really important
- ✓ You used your words,
  but they won't stop
- ✓ Someone could get hurt
- ✓ Someone is in danger
- ✓ It is not safe

Funny though, sometimes we don't tell
when we should tell.

Why is that? ☀

I definitely need to tell when I am being treated in a bad way. You would need to tell too.

There are times when I just have a gut feeling that something is not okay.

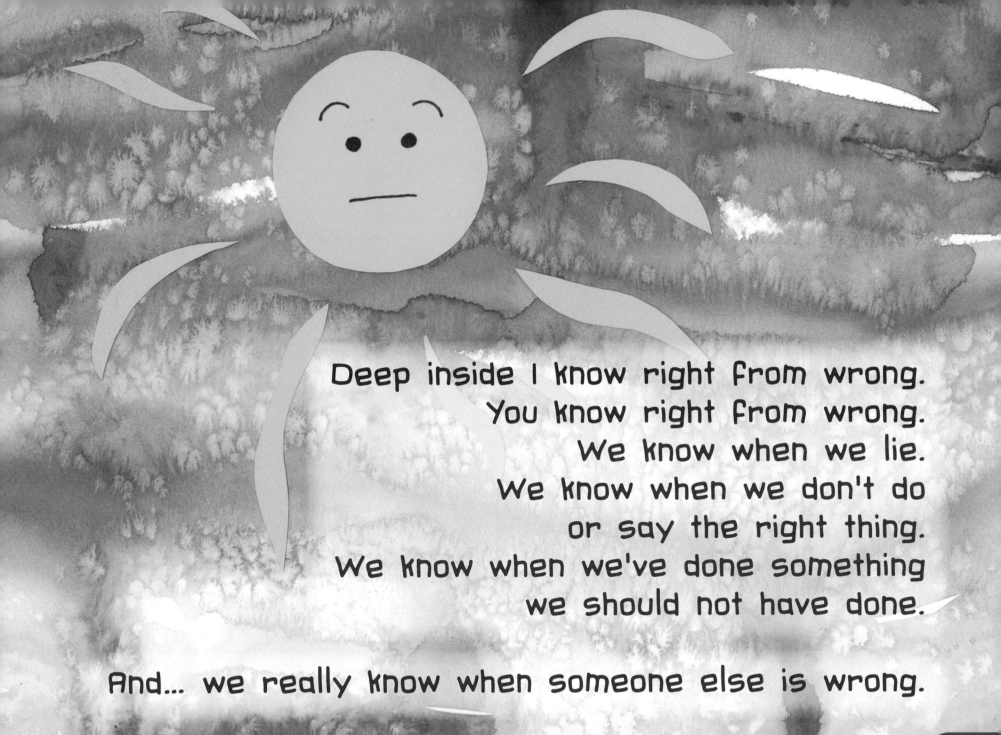

Deep inside I know right from wrong.
You know right from wrong.
We know when we lie.
We know when we don't do
or say the right thing.
We know when we've done something
we should not have done.

And... we really know when someone else is wrong.

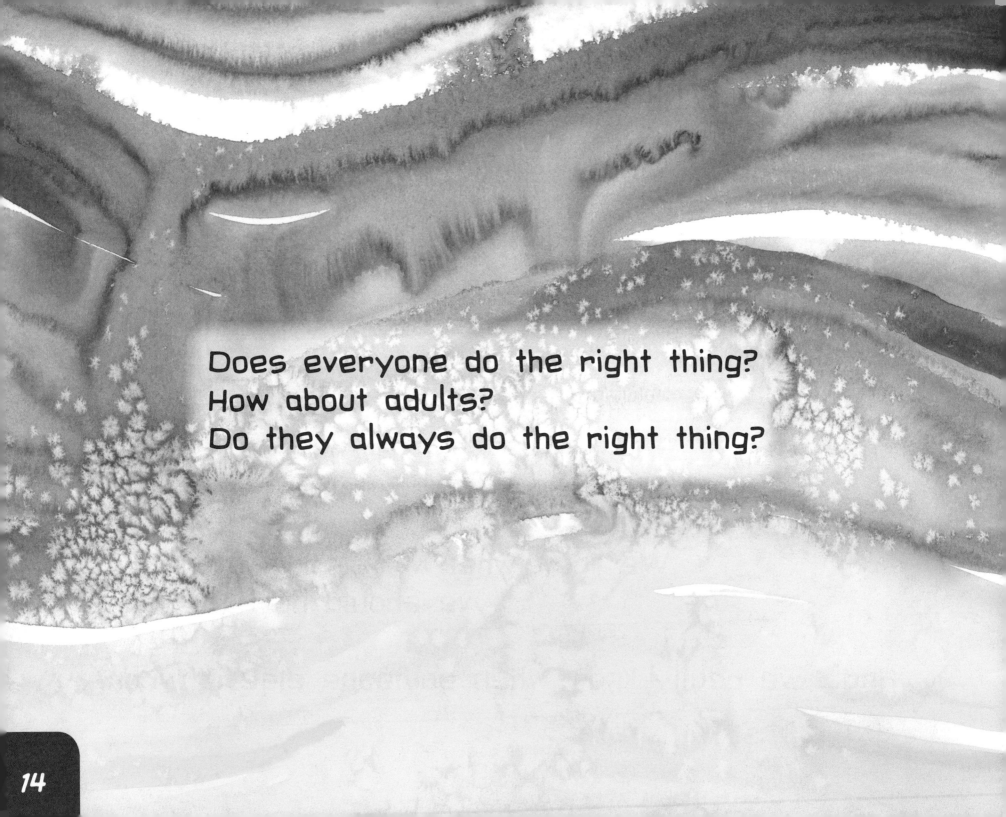

Does everyone do the right thing?
How about adults?
Do they always do the right thing?

What are some things adults do that are not okay?

15

Sometimes things might happen to us that are not right, like if someone physically hurts us.

What does it mean to be physically hurt? ✳

We could be hurt one time or several times.
This makes us scared.
It makes us feel awful inside
and hurts us on the outside.
I've felt that way before.
It makes me gloomy and sad.
This is called "physical abuse."

Sometimes we get hurt emotionally.
That means having our feelings hurt.
I've had my feelings hurt before.
That happens once-in-awhile.
But when it happens over and over again,
it needs to STOP.

This is called "emotional abuse."

There is even another abuse,
like if someone touches us
in our private areas.

Private areas are our private parts
that are covered up with our swim suits.
These are our special areas
that someone else should not be touching.

This can confuse us.
If this has happened to you,
you are not the only one.
It has happened to other kids too.
This has even happened to me.
This is called "sexual abuse."

Well... of course, there are sometimes...

Like if we have an owie or an infection in a private area, then mom, dad, or the doctor may need to check us just to keep us healthy. That's okay, that's important.

It's also not okay for us to touch
someone else's private areas either.

NO

Even if they want us to
or if they make us touch them.

That's not right.
That's not okay.

Then, we say, "NO!"

Even if someone has already touched you or made you touch them, it is **not** your fault.
It was not my fault when it happened to me.
I was feeling:
- ✓ Confused
- ✓ Scared
- ✓ Worried that if told, no one will believe me
- ✓ Guilty
- ✓ Ashamed
- ✓ Afraid I would get in trouble
- ✓ Afraid I would make someone mad
- ✓ Or...if I told, everything would change

But it needs to change! It needs to stop!
You need to tell!
Again, it is **not** your fault! ✡

People who do these things could be your age.
They could be older than you.
They could be an adult.
They could be someone really old.
You just never know.
They could be any age.
It could be someone you know
and even care a lot about.

The person who abused me was someone I knew!
It was even someone I liked and cared about!
Hardly ever would it be someone you don't know.
Like a stranger.

If you are being abused
and someone is hurting you
physically, emotionally, or touching you
in private areas, then it is time to TELL!!

24

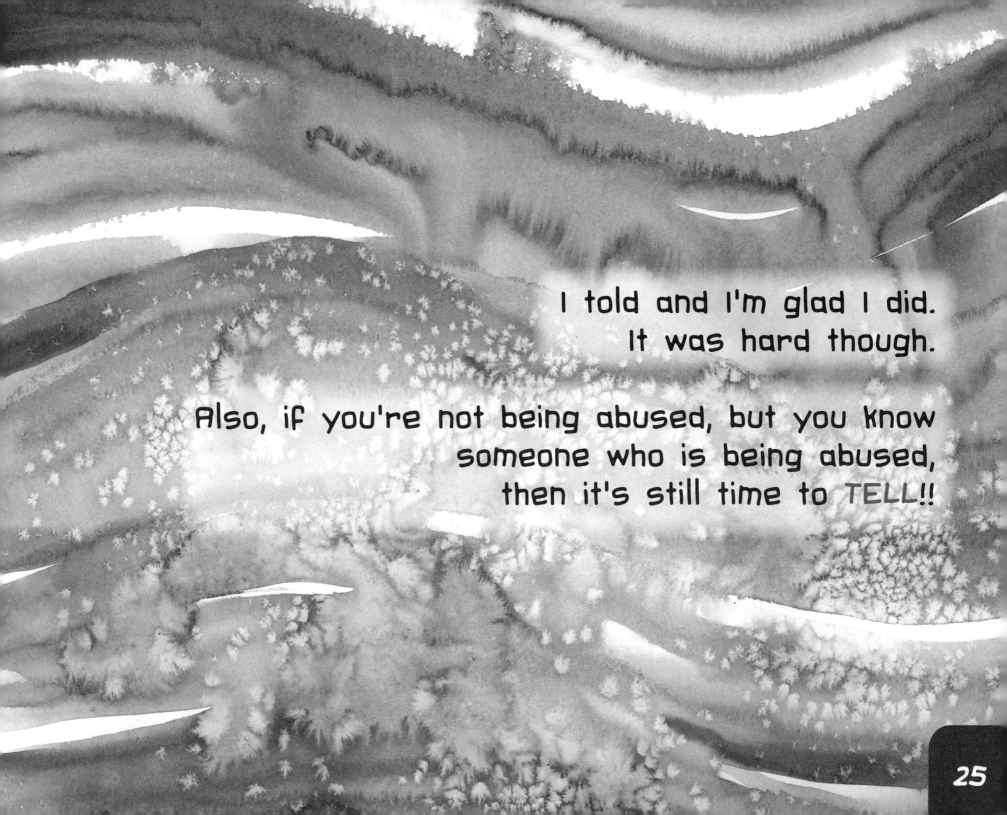

I told and I'm glad I did.
It was hard though.

Also, if you're not being abused, but you know
someone who is being abused,
then it's still time to *TELL!!*

Who do you think you could tell?
Of course... it would be someone you trust.
Like:

- ✔ An adult
- ✔ A parent
- ✔ A teacher
- ✔ A principal
- ✔ A counselor
- ✔ A doctor
- ✔ A nurse

Or...who else? ☀

TELL

I told an adult what was happening to me and they listened.
We worked things out so that I was safe.
But remember, if you tell someone and they don't do anything to help, then tell another person and keep, keep telling.

WOW! There are lots of people to help.

It is our job to tell,
even if we are threatened
or told not to tell.
Even if it means
we could lose a friend.
Even if it means
someone will get mad.

If we don't tell, things won't
stop and it needs to stop!
I told, and I'm glad I did because it stopped!

By the way, what does threatened mean?

Sometimes we are even told
to keep secrets we shouldn't keep.

There are some good secrets
and there are not good secrets.

A secret for a birthday party
is a good secret.
Like a fun surprise!

But if someone is treating you badly
or abusing you and
they tell you not to tell anyone,
you need to tell anyway.
Then, it is not a good secret.

I was told to not tell, but I told anyway.
Sometimes it is hard, but we need to be brave,
strong and tell when we should.
I had to be brave and strong to tell.
You can tell too.

It's not okay to be hurt.

I care about you and so do lots of other people!

Hey, so what did we learn about tattling and telling?

You tell me.

What did you learn?

Appendix

Page 9

Two strategies that you can use in your school district
1. Look at Them, Name it, Walk Away
   - ✓ Look at Them- means look them in the eye
   - ✓ Name it- name what they are doing
     (For example: that's mean, that's rude, that's not nice, that's name calling, etc.)
   - ✓ Walk Away- even if they keep yelling at you or asking you to come back, keep walking away
     (If they follow you, go get help)
2. Stop, Walk, Talk
   - ✓ Tell them to stop
   - ✓ If they don't stop, walk away
   - ✓ Tell someone

Page 11

Why is it that sometimes we don't tell when we should tell?
1. Mention how little kids love to tattle on each other. Then, there is some unknown age where it changes, as they get older, and then they don't tell when they should tell. Some responses could be:
   - ✓ Afraid of retaliation
   - ✓ Don't want to be involved
   - ✓ Think it's no big deal, when it is a big deal
   - ✓ Have been threatened to not tell
   - ✓ Fearful of getting someone in trouble
   - ✓ Fearful of losing a friend

Page 15

What are some things adults do that are not okay?
1. Kids will usually answer this truthfully and straight forward. Here are some possible answers:
   - ✓ Smoking
   - ✓ Abuse
   - ✓ Breaking the law
   - ✓ Drinking
     (When they talk about drinking, you may want to share that drinking alcohol is not against the law, as long as someone is old enough. It's not okay if someone has had too much to drink. Tell children, they probably know when someone has had too much to drink. Drinking changes that person's behavior and they may not be safe.)

Appendix

Page 16

What does it mean to be physically hurt?

1. Children have many different answers to this question. It is important to define "physically hurt."
   - ✓ Physically hurt is hurting the body that results in pain.
2. Discuss with the students that there is a fine line between discipline and abuse. Children are disciplined differently depending on their parent's expectations but for some it can go too far. Then, it becomes physical abuse.
   - ✓ A spanking hurts but it shouldn't leave marks or bruises.

Page 21

If a child has been abused, speaking up about it is one of the hardest things for them to do. We have to give them the support and tools to come forward. Share with students that if someone is being abused and they never say anything, the abuse won't stop and it needs to stop. The abuser is likely to continue to hurt someone else and not just them. When they speak up, they may be protecting another child.

Page 23

Facts and Statistics About Sex Offenses

1. 1 out of 4 girls and 1 out of 6 boys will experiene some form of sexual abuse before the age of 18.
   (CDCP, 2005)
2. In as many as 93 percent of child sexual cases, the child knows the person that commits the abuse.
   (Douglas, 2009)
3. 23% of reported cases of child sexual abuse are perpetrated by individuals under the age of 18.
   (Snyder, 2000)

Page 26

Brainstorm more ideas with the child/children about who are people we can trust and tell.

Page 28

What does threatened mean?

1. Threat- An expression of intention to inflict evil, injury or damage.
   (Explain how damaging threats are. Encourage them to tell immediately when they have been threatened. Discuss the severity of threats. One uses threats to control, to prolong a situation, or to escape consequences.)

Tips for Parents

Building Skills with Your Child

- ✓ Early on, teach your child to speak up if something isn't right.

- ✓ Be open and honest when communicating so they feel they can come to you no matter what has been happening.

- ✓ Encourage and teach them to talk about how they feel. In everyday occurrences, share feelings. For example: "I'm tired today, how are you feeling?" Expand your child's vocabulary.

Observing Your Child's Behaviors *(These observations are not necessarily indications of abuse but could be)*

- ✓ Keep an eye open for changes in your child. For example: are they quieter than usual, are they sad, do they avoid talking to you and/or has their behavior changed (either more active than usual, maybe more frustrated, quick to anger, changes in eating habits either over eating or under eating)?

- ✓ Notice their actions as they play. Are there inappropriate behaviors, and/or words?

- ✓ Are they not wanting to leave you?

If Your Child Has Been Abused

- ✓ Do your best to not react in a strong emotional way.

- ✓ Listen to the child and hear them completely before responding.

- ✓ Show them that you believe them so they can trust you.

- ✓ Do not put blame on yourself.

- ✓ Be supportive and strong for them.

- ✓ Don't treat abuse as a deep dark secret.

- ✓ Your child will need to feel supported and told over and over that what has happened was not their fault.

- ✓ Be open and honest about what has happened with your child.

- ✓ Share information with people who need to know but don't talk about it constantly or in front of your child.

Tips for Parents

Help for You and Your Child

✓ Give your child an opportunity to talk about what has happened in a safe environment. For example: a place they feel comfortable and a quiet place without interruptions.

✓ Counseling provides support but take the time to choose someone who would be a good fit for you and your child. Ask your school counselor for recommendations.

✓ Contact the **National Child Abuse Hotline (1-800-422-4453)** for more information and help.

✓ Take advantage of your local mental health professionals. They are trained to help parents and children work through the abuse.

✓ Find help through school counselors, social workers, principals, teachers, doctors, nurses, police officers, etc.

Sources

1. Centers for Disease Control and Prevention. (2005). Adverse Childhood Experiences Study: Data and Statistics. Atlanta, GA: Centers for Disease Control and Prevention, National Center for Injury Prevention and Control. Retrieved July 9, 2013 from: http://www.cdc.gov/nccdphp/ace/prevalence.htm

2. Douglas, Emily and D. Finkelhor, Childhood sexual abuse fact sheet, http://www.unh.edu/ccrc/factsheet/pdf/childhoodSexualAbuseFactSheet.pdf, Crimes Against Children Research Center, May 2005 Durham, NH: Retrieved July 23, 2013 from: http://www.stopitnow.org/csa_fact_who_abuse

3. Snyder, H. N. (2000). Sexual assault of young children as reported to law enforcement: Victim, incident, and offender characteristics. Washington, DC: U.S. Department of Justice, Office of Justice Programs, Bureau of Justice Statistics. Retrieved July 9, 2013 from http://www.ojp.usdoj.gov/bjs/pub/pdf/saycrle.pdf

About the Author, Julie Mendenhall, B.S./M.A.

Julie is a wife, mother, grandmother, author, musician, and an educator.
She holds a credential in special education/elementary education
and has a masters degree in counseling.
In her 38 plus years of experience she has obtained
a wealth of knowledge and experience.
Julie is currently a counselor for an elementary school,
living with her family in Grand Junction, Colorado
and plans to continue writing for children.
Julie's work can be found at juliemendenhall.webs.com.

About the Illustrator, Maja Sommersted, B.A.

Maja Sommersted is a professional artist who enjoys working in a variety of media.
The illustrations in this book were done combining watercolor and collage.
Maja is originally from Denmark and as a child she lived in Africa and
England before her family settled in the United States.
Maja teaches art at an Elementary School
and lives in Colorado with her husband and three daughters.
Maja's work can be found at majasommersted.com.

Look for These and Other Related Resources from YouthLight

Brad Learns How to Take a Bite Out of Meanness

Being Positive and Firm When Dealing with Teasing and Name Calling

By: Susan Bowman

This colorfully illustrated story introduces Brad, an unusual shark, who doesn't "fit in" with the other sharks. He is teased and called names by other sea creatures because he doesn't fit the reputation of being a shark. So he tries to not hang around the other sharks hoping this will make a difference. But the teasing continues. He finally turns to his only friend Kia, a humpback whale, who tells him that he should not try to change who he is just to have friends.

Brad learns that, "True friends are those who like you for who you are and accept you no matter how different you are." Kia tells him that it's important to not respond to meanness with meanness. It is important to be positive. You can be firm with others when you need to, but not mean. When Brad tries these new skills, he learns that when being teased, being positive but firm is a better way to respond. He eventually gains new friends and earns respect for his positive and friendly attitude.

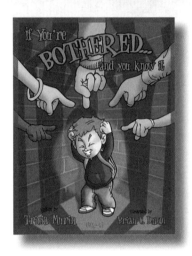

If You're Bothered and You Know It

By: Tricia Murin

A staggering amount of children are afraid to attend school in fear of being bullied. *If Your Bothered and You Know It* teaches students confidence-building strategies to help them stand up for themselves and not tolerate bothersome behaviors that are repetitive and may turn into bullying behaviors. Students are taught 5 ways to stop the bullying before it happens. These strategies are incorporated into a song called *If You're Bothered and You Know it* which is based on the popular tune *If You're Happy and You Know It Clap Your Hands.* This book is easy to read and easy for the students to relate to and includes follow-up activities.

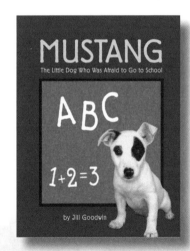

Mustang, The Little Dog Who Was Afraid to Go to School

By Jill Goodman

This endearing story of a scared little puppy was written to help children face their fears about school. Without timely intervention these fears can escalate into school phobia.

Mustang will assist children in using positive self-talk to overcome any fears they might have about school. In the process, they will learn a valuable skill that will help them overcome other new challenges as they encounter them.

P.O. Box 115 ☼ Chapin, SC 29036  youth light inc. 800.209.9774 ☼ yl@youthlightbooks.com ☼ www.youthlight.com

Look for these and Other Related Resources from YouthLight

My Daddy Is In Jail

By: Janet Bender

My Daddy is in Jail is a long overdue resource for helping children cope with the incarceration of a loved one. It includes a read-aloud story discussion guide caregiver suggestions and optional small group counseling activities. With this book helping professionals and other caring adults will find themselves better equipped to provide information and support to these vulnerable children and their families.

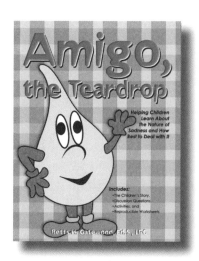

Amigo, the Teardrop

Helping Children Learn About the Nature of Sadness and How Best to Deal With It

By: Betts Gatewood

Can tears be our friends? Our friendly teardrop Amigo wants us to realize that they can be! This endearing story helps children think through various events we cannot always predict or control that might bring sadness to us. Amigo helps children understand that there are different degrees of sadness and that we all feel this way sometimes. He gives positive and specific ideas of things we can do to help us feel better and he gives us permission to cry! Amigo ends his adventure by reminding children that people even cry sometimes when they are happy - a true sign that teardrops are our friends!

The Big Red Bird and the Red Feather Game

A Book About Calming and Self-Control Skills for Children When They Are Upset

By: Cindy Wetzel

The Big Red Bird is a delightful caring feathered friend. In this story, she becomes very upset after she notices some children yelling, arguing and name calling at one another. But the The Big Red Bird knew a wonderful skill to help herself calm down so she could think better about doing the right thing. Then she teaches the children how to use this skill using some of her red feathers.

This book provides a fun, unforgettable way children can improve their self-regulation when they are upset, or feel an urge to act out. It is a valuable resource for children who have difficulties with impulse control.

Included are several worksheets at the end to reinforce the lesson. The book also includes game instructions and a package with some real red feathers for "The Red Feather Game." This can be played by one or more children and will enhance the techniques learned from the story.

800.209.9774 ☼ yl@youthlightbooks.com ☼ www.youthlight.com

youth light inc.

P.O. Box 115 ☼ Chapin, SC 29036